Lucky, a Dogs Tale

Dave Lodge

Pixel tweaks
PUBLICATIONS

Published in 2016
© Copyright Dave Lodge

ISBN: 978-0-9956190-3-6

Cover and Book interior Design by Russell Holden
www.pixeltweakspublications.com

Pixel ❈ tweaks
PUBLICATIONS

All rights reserved without limiting the rights under copyright reserved above, no parts of this publication may be reproduced, stored in or introduced into a retrieval system, or transmitted in any form, or by any means (electronic, mechanical, photocopying, recording or otherwise) without the prior written permission of both the copyright owner and the publisher of this book, Dave Lodge

Acknowledgements

My thanks for the help, support and memories go to Margaret, Peter and Lynda Leonard, Joan and Pat Whelan, their dog Rocky and Dennis and Christine Brown (who also supplied the images at the back of the book and I thank them for the lovely memories they preserved on film). My thanks also go to Russell Holden, who for the third time now has produced a simply remarkable book on my behalf.

This book is dedicated to all the pets we've had the privilege of sharing our home with over the years – Lucky, Whiskey, Rex x 2, Max, Rusty, Buster, Gyp, Mickey, Lassie, Bruno, Oscar and Brandy. We are grateful they have shared the lives of Margaret and me along the way.

Contents

Chapter 1 1
Chapter 2 6
Chapter 3 12
Chapter 4 17
Chapter 5 26
Chapter 6 32
Chapter 7 35
Chapter 8 46
Chapter 9 53
Chapter 10 59
Final word 63

Chapter 1

This is my life story. My name is Lucky, at least that's what everyone calls me! Maybe when you read my story, you'll understand why. There's just one thing I need to tell you just one thing before I continue ... I am a dog.

"What?" I hear you say, "a dog?"

Yes, a dog – a dog can have a life story, can't he? Enough rhetorical questions, I feel a philosophical argument coming on so I will just tell the story, then let you decide the answer for yourselves.

My earliest memory is of finding myself surrounded by others like me – my brothers and sisters; we were all small and vulnerable as we couldn't see where we were or what we were doing. We kept falling over each other and bumping into things ... it was very chaotic. We knew we were related because we could smell a familiar scent. We would all crawl around and find a bigger version of ourselves. It felt warm and safe being beside this bigger version of us and we would lie close, snuggle up and suckle a warm, sweet liquid from her. I'd heard it called 'milk'; it was delicious, and I liked it.

Over the days and weeks that followed, things were changing around me. I began to see my siblings and with this improved vision we even stopped bumping into each other. I also learned that the bigger version of us who cared for us and supplied the lovely milk was our mother. We seemed to be getting better at moving around and as time went by I started to get to know my surroundings and understand that I was different from my siblings, who I was hearing referred to variously as 'pups', 'animals' and 'dogs'.

Unlike my well-proportioned and frisky siblings, I was clumsy and slow. My head was a big as my body, and I had huge feet that made me trip over. This clumsiness caused me many problems, so I wasn't getting as much food as my speedy siblings.

Our pack share space with a couple of large two-legged creatures, who as we grew bigger, spent more and more time with us. This wasn't a pleasant experience, at times as they were very rough when they handled us and would make a lot of noise. One noise was very loud - it was called 'shouting' and because of my clumsiness, it was usually aimed in my direction.

As time went by I recognised many of the sounds I heard and found they were a form of communication although I only understood sounds used by the four-legged creatures like me; our 'yelps' and 'barks' had different pitches to mean different things.

The large two-legged creatures had a very different way of communicating with each other. Their sounds, which at first I thought were just loud noises, turned out to be instructions and commands meaning they wanted us to "sit" "lie down" or "shut up". I slowly began to understand that some of these words were being aimed at me. Sadly as well as the usual commands I heard one of them say,

"Ugly little devil, all head, and feet"

And I knew it was me he was talking about because I wasn't as well liked as the other pups.

My siblings were treated more kindly than me and the Masters, (as the two-legged ones were called), picked them up and cuddled them all the time. I was never picked up and cuddled.

Then came the day that would change my life forever. It was only a few weeks after I was born and I heard one of the Masters saying;

"It's time some of these pups were gone, they're nearly four weeks old".

Then looking in my direction, he said:

"We need to get rid of that ugly one".

"Right," said the other, who picked me up and threw me roughly in to a cardboard box.

I was then plonked inside another even bigger box ... a metal box with windows, wheels and doors.

"What a strange kennel, with a funny smell" I thought.

Suddenly this kennel with wheels made a loud noise unlike any I had heard before; then I felt it moving.

I was whining and crying – terrified as the box on wheels went faster and faster. I tried to get out of the box. I was so scared and couldn't help wetting myself.

"Right!" I heard one of the Masters shout, "That's it; I've had enough, he's useless to us."

I felt the big kennel slow down, and suddenly a rough hand grabbed me. At that point I was sick, the door opened, and I was hurled into the open air, eventually landing with a bump. I slid and stumbled along the ground before eventually coming to a stop.

I just lead there motionless, trying to make sense of what had happened, I was hurt all over and crying pitifully. Eventually, I mustered some strength, staggered to my feet and tried to wander off. I was dizzy and sore, moving aimlessly.

I felt myself being picked up; I struggled and cried in fear. I soon found myself in a yet another kennel on wheels, with a different smell.

My intuition told me I was being held by a female. Her mate was driving the kennel. I was in a panic and trembling, afraid of the unpleasantness that was bound to come next.

So what a surprise when she lifted me up higher so that we were looking into each other's faces and said in a gentle, calming voice,

"Oh you poor little love, don't be frightened, you will be alright now".

She lowered me back down on to her lap; Then I heard the other one speak,

"Let's take him home and get him checked out."

"Home!" I yelped, "Home! I don't want to go!"

Neither of them seemed to be listening, so I repeated myself over and over again.

"What's he yelping about?" asked the male,

"I don't know" replied the female, "I think, he is probably frightened."

I settled down on the female's lap, and I must have fallen asleep because when I stirred I felt warm and comfortable and my nervousness seemed to have subsided. The kennel on wheels had stopped, and the male said:

"Okay Margaret bring him in."

I looked around as Margaret carried me down a path, saying to me

"Look, this will be your garden now and at the end of the path is your new house."

I felt an unfamiliar contentment wash over me, and I resolved to do everything I could to ensure that these two people would want me to stay with them.

Chapter 2

As I settled in my new home, I got used to hearing the two-legged ones call each other by name. The man is called David, and the lady is Margaret. They had a discussion about what to call me. David said,

"I think we should call him Lucky because we are lucky to have him, and he is lucky to be here after being thrown out of a moving car." Margaret agreed.

So, Lucky it was. I soon learned that I was supposed to 'come' when I heard my name, but that doesn't mean I that I always did.

At first David & Margaret tried me with various things to eat, but the only thing I could manage was water and milk. Margaret went out and bought some puppy food. She put some in a bowl and it smelled lovely, but I didn't know what to do with it. Then she had a brilliant idea; she sat on the floor, so she was close to me, got a wooden spoon and put some of this stuff on it, holding it out to me. I sniffed and licked at it, it tasted great, and I was able to suck at the spoon which pulled the food into my mouth, I moved it around in my mouth, and it tasted lovely, then I swallowed, and I soon felt full and sleepy and dozed off. Margaret fed me like that for weeks, in fact, for the next sixteen years I would get her to feed me like that, just for fun, every now and again, it was like a special bond that we shared between us.

David took me for a check-up to McDonald's the vets. I didn't like it much – as we went in it smelt of bad, stale, animal smells and there was one particularly horrible smell that I instinctively knew ... the smell of death! I heard a woman crying, her cat who she loved had been put to sleep, and she was going to miss it. I was really frightened and leant against David's leg. After a while we met a nice man called Patrick, David told me he was my vet and would look after me whenever I was poorly. I liked him; David was talking to him about me, and then I had an examination. Patrick gave me an injection, a sharp thing in the back of my neck which made me yelp. David explained to me that it was to protect me against something called Parvo, I didn't know what that was, but I understood it was part of taking care of me. Even though I liked Patrick, I was glad I'd only have to visit him once a year throughout my life. The vets was a place I would have preferred not to go.

While we were there, Patrick told David that I was only about five weeks old and way too young to have left my mother.

"Ah," said Margaret, "that's why he can't eat properly".

Whilst we were there Margaret asked about something called 'castration'. I didn't know what castration was but as David was pulling a wincing face I assumed it probably wasn't good. Patrick told Margaret that it was something responsible owners usually arranged for their dogs, but that because it looked like I was going to grow & grow he wouldn't do it until I was two years old ... after that there'd be no nights out courting for me!

Everything at the new house was wonderful and new, I had important things to do in the garden, I had to play in the bushes, dig up plants and bury bones. I hadn't quite got the idea of the last one. I would dig a hole, put the bone in the hole and then walk away. David would always say, "he doesn't know he has to cover the bone with soil".

I thought "If I do that I won't be able to find it when I want it". I never did cover the bones up, nor did I ever go back for them. I liked the idea of these bones, but I wasn't sure why I got them.

Life in the new house was great. I wasn't the only four-leg in there, though. There was another creature, she had soft fur, was very fussy and spoke a different language! Her name was Whiskey, and she was a Tortoiseshell cat – she looked lovely, but that didn't stop me chasing her up the stairs. I didn't know it then, but Whiskey would be like a mother to me, and we would become great friends.

Whiskey's story was similar to mine. David had found her under the garden shed, and she was very small and very hungry. He'd brought her into the house, and Margaret fed her chicken. She never grew to be very big, but she grew to be a lovely cat and was active and healthy.

She stayed with David and Margaret; they loved her, and she loved them. She would often jump up on David's knee then get up on his shoulder and go to sleep on his neck. The whole environment seemed just right for a happy life.

David would go off to work every day, and I'd spend my days with Margaret. So when he came home from work at night, I made sure

I was waiting at the gate. I'd get up on my hind legs and put my front paws on him as high as they could reach, which was just below his knee and just look up at him. He liked this and always picked me up and made a fuss of me. Of course, as the years went by and I grew I still greeted him in the same way, but my paws would be draped over his shoulders, he couldn't pick me up anymore, but he still made a fuss of me.

One day David and Margaret had gone out and left me to look after the house. I was feeling a bit bored on my own and after having a look around the living room thought I would have a quick chew on the corner of the armchair to pass the time. It was great fun, the stuffing from the chair was flying everywhere. I went from the chair to the sofa and tore it to bits too. I looked for dessert and wandered towards David's recliner, but I was so tired by then I just curled up on it and went to sleep instead.

When David and Margaret returned I jumped down and ran to them with my tail wagging, I was sure they'd be so happy at my hard work. They were looking around the room just shaking their heads in disbelief. I knew they were pleased! I couldn't wait for them to go out again so I could do something equally impressive for them.

The next time they went out I pulled books out of the bookcase and tore them to shreds. Paper and cardboard were everywhere. When David and Margaret came back in, I rushed to them full of excitement; They looked round, saying,

"Well, at least he doesn't do things by half".

Then David said as he was picking up the torn paper,

"You know Margaret it's funny, but it seems he is partial to destroying your things. He tore up your chair and the sofa but left my recliner alone, the only books he has torn up are your Catherine Cookson novels. I think we need to get him something to keep him occupied when we are out".

"Good idea," said Margaret. "If he keeps on the way he is he will destroy the whole house".

Soon I had been given all sorts of things to play with, toys that squeaked, bouncy balls, rubber bones and pulling ropes. The pulling me were my favourite, I would hold my end of the rope in my mouth and try to drag David out of his chair while shaking my head vigorously from side to side, I always won – I have incredibly powerful jaws. I knew he let me win, and he always told me how strong I was. I got stronger and stronger, all the exercise I was getting was doing me good.

For the first time in my life I felt I belonged, I felt part of the family and life was good. There was food whenever I needed it and always fresh water for me to drink.

I was getting plenty of something called 'exercise. Three times a day I'd be taken out for a nice walk. They were only short walks, at first, but as I got bigger they got longer and longer. The only drawback was I had to wear a collar and lead when we went for these walks. I wasn't keen on this and used to jump around and try to get the lead out of Margaret or David's hand.

Going on walks was my precious time with just David and Margaret, we didn't take Whiskey with us, even though I wanted to because she was my companion. Whiskey preferred to be more solitary; she would go off and exercise alone. Having said that we were always pleased to see each other when we got back.

I also find out from listening to Margaret and David that I was part Newfoundland and part Labrador. Apparently, this combination meant that I would grow up a very big dog. Margaret asked David,

"How big?"

He replied, "We will need a saddle for this one."

I did grow to be as enormous as predicted and despite my clumsiness and lolloping size they loved me for who I was, they'd say 'Lucky is just himself, there is no other like him, he is one in a million'. I liked that ... but I never did get the saddle I was promised!

Chapter 3

As the weeks went by and I grew bigger and stronger something new was added to the outings called 'training'. This was very exciting; we went onto a big green space they called a field – they would let me off the lead, and I'd run free. They'd throw a ball for me – the idea was I should catch it in my mouth and take it back to them so that it could be thrown again. Sometimes, to be mischevious, I just kept running around pretending not to hear when they called my name; it was a good game and made me laugh watching Margaret and David running around trying to catch me.

My training was very frustrating at times for David. There were too many distractions, other dogs that I wanted to say hello to, cats that were hiding in the bushes that needed chasing, other dog's balls that I thought I could catch and run after.

Probably the final straw with my behaviour came as David and I came as we were coming back from a walk one evening. I was quite tired as we had been running around for over an hour and I was looking forward to a nice cold drink of water and a lie-down. We were almost home when I saw something that meant there was more fun for me to have.

Squirrels and cats were in my opinion put on this earth for the sole purpose of being chased by me, so when I saw a cat I had to go off in hot pursuit. As I sprang into action, I heard David call me back.

"Ha," I thought, "no chance". He kept shouting, the cat kept running, and so did I. The cat turned down his garden path as I was gaining on it, so I hurtled down the path towards the open back door just as the cat ran through it.

The crafty cat may have thought it had reached safety. He ran in to the living room and jumped on an armchair with a meow of relief. He was suddenly brought back to reality though as a massive black dog jumped on the armchair too. As he jumped three feet in the air in surprise on to the sofa, I followed him. The lady of the house was as surprised by all this as the cat and could only watch in disbelief as the cat sprang onto the dining table then up onto the top of a display cabinet with me in hot pursuit. It was at this point things went wrong for me. The lovely clean tablecloth the lady had placed on the table was sliding under my feet - 'oh-oh' I thought as I landed on the floor with a big thud tangled in the tablecloth surrounded by plates and cutlery on the floor around me,

By this time David had arrived and got hold of me. He was apologising profusely; the lady was saying,

"Just get him out"!

I looked up to see the cat laughing at me. I felt a complete fool. When we got home, David told Margaret what had happened. Then he had to go back and apologise properly (to the lady ... not to the cat I hope).

The lady had been very pleasant and forgiving; she had seen the funny side of the incident, saying, "Not to worry, dogs will chase cats".

I had to be put back on to the lead after this incident for future walks, as David said, this time, we'd been lucky that the lady was so nice, but I couldn't be trusted. The trouble was I was having great fun, and I didn't think I needed to pay attention to David or Margaret. I would soon find out that I was wrong.

One evening after they had taken a long time to catch me David was getting exasperated. I heard him say,

"This is pointless, we can't even get him to come back to us when we're in the garden, so what chance do we have of controlling him in an open space, we need a new plan."

It wasn't long until I found out what the new plan was. David would take me out for my first walk every day an hour earlier; that meant he would have to get up an hour earlier for work. He said to me,

"The thing is Lucky, I'm hoping that there will be fewer distractions for you, then we will see if you can concentrate."

I liked this about him, the way he spoke to me as though he knew I understood him, Margaret spoke to me in the same way, and I was coming to the conclusion that I had found my true home.

I realised on the first morning there was a flaw in David's training plan. We walked onto the field; it was dark – very dark, I am dark, I am jet black. So I thought he won't be able to see me, I smiled as I looked up at him, as he was preparing to take my lead off. David smiled back at me and released me, and I raced away. In a couple of strides, I was at full pace, and I was sure I had disappeared from view. "Ha Ha," I thought "I fooled you", I ran and ran, I was happy to be free.

It was very quiet and dark, and I stopped running in a straight line and began running round in circles, wait I thought it is too quiet, why can't I hear David's voice calling for me? I started to panic and to sniff the ground for my own scent, I picked it up and trotted back the way I had come.

After what seemed like an eternity I saw David's shape loom up out of the darkness, I ran towards him jumping up with excitement shouted 'I thought I had lost you!' although to him, I suppose I was just barking, even so, I knew he understood.

He calmed me down and as we walked along together, he smiled and looked down at me saying, 'I'm not as stupid as you thought am I?' he asked. I knew then that he really did understand me and we were the same.

I suddenly felt an overwhelming feeling that I instinctively knew was love, and I knew it was reciprocated, this was the beginning of the relationship that would last my lifetime. We had become great friends but more than that I realised that we were a family, basically David and Margaret were my mum and dad, and I loved them both. Indeed Margaret would say things like, "Your dad will be home soon". He would say to me, "Your mum is getting your tea ready".

We were a real family now, and Whiskey was like my sister. So I loved her too. Whiskey and I spent a lot of time together when dad and mum were out. This was our quiet time, and I have to say we spent most of it lying on the sofa together asleep. But home is where you relax, isn't it? Life was good and unbelievably it was getting better.

Soon a whole year had passed (that's a human year) and as I had been with David and Margaret for 12 months I had something called a birthday! Because they didn't know the exact date of my birth, they would celebrate it on the day we all got together, 3rd of April. It was a lovely surprise and apparently it would happen every year. It was a great day; they made a fuss of me, and I got gifts – a lovely new ball with a bell in it and some very tasty chewy sticks. Whiskey's birthday was on the 10th of November, and that was a great day too. I'm not sure that Whiskey and I thought about our birthdays coming round, but we liked the fact that we were part of a family.

Chapter 4

I looked forward to my walks, and our training was continuing. David would say to me,

"We are learning from, and about, each other."

That told me that we were equals – amazing! Other dogs I met when we were out told me it was most unusual to be an equal. Usually, dogs were called 'pets' and had a master and or a mistress. Even the ones that were well treated were told what to do. I felt very proud – I was family, and just as important, I was an equal.

On our outings things were going very well, David had endless patience with me. He told me that he hated to shout at anyone or anything so if he wanted me to come to him he would make a whistling sound with his lips.

David would walk along, and I would run ahead. He would whistle, and I ran back to him, then he would let me go on again. We'd change it a bit, and he would whistle so I would still run back to him then bit by bit we would add more things to this repertoire. One of them was 'sit' then 'walk on together', then it was 'sit', and David would walk on, and I would stay, watching, he would then stop, tap the outside of his leg and I would run to him sit again, and then we would walk on again. I wasn't always quick to comply, but as I said David was patient, and we just tried the instruction again until we got it right. Soon things were working well, and my responses were almost instantaneous, although there were times when I forgot if I was following a new scent, which seemed really interesting.

Unfortunately sometimes on our walk we'd run into the odd problem – usually not of our making. For example, there was a Dalmatian that unbeknown to us was also being taken on walks along the route that we used. This dog, unlike others of is breed, was very unpleasant and would fight viciously with any dog that was unfortunate enough to be anywhere in his vicinity. His owners suffered most from his behaviour due to a number of vet's bills they incurred due to the Dalmatians attacks on other dogs.

This dog was about eighteen months older than me and a good size. I was growing fast but I was in no way equipped for the unbelievable ferocity of the first attack when it came.

One day dad and I were out walking; our confidence in each other had grown more and more by this time, and I was probably too far in front of him as I walked through the wood into a clearing. Suddenly without warning, something hit me. It was like being hit by a ton of bricks; I was flung through the air, and I landed with a thump on my back. I was stunned and completely disorientated and given no time to recover. I heard a most terrible noise; I didn't know it was possible to growl, snarl, and bark at the same time – but the large, snapping teeth that were surrounded by black and white spotted skin seemed to have all these sounds emitting from them at the same time.

I was paralysed with fear, and I felt myself being bitten and this monster, was salivating all over me. I couldn't breathe, and I was shaking violently. I could hear shouting. I recognised dad's, but the other must have been the monster's owner. Dad's voice wasn't as loud, and he seemed to be in control. The Dalmatian's owner appeared to be hysterical, as out of control as his dog.

I heard dad say,

"Call your dog off, get hold of him, do something"!

The guy replied,

"You have got to be joking; I can't go near him when he's like this."

Time seemed to stand still, and suddenly the monster let me go. I looked up, and dad had hold of him by its collar. It was still snarling and slavering. In a split second it leapt up in the air, and I thought, it was going to rip dad's throat out! I blinked my eyes and in that second everything was quiet, the Dalmatian was on all four feet standing quietly on the ground, dad's other hand was in its mouth. He took it out and told the Dalmatian's owner to put his lead on, NOW! The guy obeyed, Saying,

"I don't believe it, your hand isn't even scratched, how did you do that"? "I don't know" dad replied, "It's something my Grandda taught me, he told me that when it finds your hand in its mouth, the dog is so surprised, it just doesn't bite you, so I just did it, I was lucky I guess".

The other guy was very chatty now, he didn't understand why his dog was like this, he is lovely at home with the family.

"Maybe", replied dad as he knelt down stroking me, "Just try and avoid us in future".

dad checked me over and surprisingly I was unhurt, He helped me calm down, and we carried on with our walk. As we walked, he told me some wise words ...

"Remember Lucky empty vessels make the most noise, the more people shout, the less you should be frightened of them, they are only shouting because they are insecure and unsure of themselves. Dogs are the same, and this one was so busy slavering and snarling he didn't manage to break the skin when he bit you. You were more frightened than hurt. There is no shame in being frightened, I get frightened but, we have to try to be brave when we are frightened and then these people have no power over us".

I never forgot what he said, and I never barked except to show that I was happy and I never even threatened to bite anyone. I think I enjoyed life more because of this.

Dad was very fond of saying things which made sense, and he said that he tried to live his life by these sayings. His favourite was,

"It's not how many times you get knocked down; your life will be judged by how many times you get back up".

I have thought about this, and it doesn't always have to be physically knocked down. It can bad things happening in your life, and People look at how you cope with this stuff, and they judge you by that.

Another regular meeting on our walks was with a Weimaraner. This dog would come up as friendly as you like and then suddenly attack me. Again not typical behaviour for the breed. We always seemed to meet him on narrow tracks through the trees so that I couldn't avoid him. He used his sheer size and weight to bowl me over then he would stand with both his front paws on my chest, looking down at me. This apparently was his normal greeting to any dog he met when out walking.

I think I was supposed to be intimidated by this but I was growing fast, very strong and with what I had heard dad saying, I felt I should be able to stand up for myself. With this in mind, I resolved that I would. Sure enough, the next time we met he came hurtling at me, I am not sure what happened next or how I came to do what I did. As he came up on me somehow I ducked under him, grabbed one of his legs and heaved upwards, he spun over and landed on his back. I very slowly put one paw on his chest and looked down at him then turned and walked slowly back to dad.

The owners of the Weimaraner spoke, "He's in shock he won't get up, he is trembling". Dad knelt down beside their dog, and he stroked until it calmed down. It got up and stood to look at me. Then dad said very quietly, "Now you know how all the other people who walked their dogs here have felt for a very long time". He went on to say, "I don't know how Lucky did that, I am sorry he felt it was necessary." We walked away.

I am pleased to say that the Weimaraner and I became good friends and were always glad to see each other when out walking. I wish the same could have been said of the Dalmatian. We just gave each other a wide berth. Sadly I heard that after a particularly vicious attack on another dog he had to be 'put down', I wasn't sure what that meant at the time, but I never saw him again.

One thing I do know is that after my incident with the Weimaraner, I never had another fight with a dog or had a problem with any aggression. Dad said it was because I had a quiet presence, so other dogs knew that I was in control. He said he was always very proud of me, I was always very proud of him.

Another amazing thing that happened around this time. I saw snow for the first time! It was incredible. White flakes were falling from the sky, sticking to the ground. As I watched through the French windows, the snow was getting deeper and deeper. I was very excited – so much so that mum and dad let me out in to the snowy garden. I ran here and there jumping and dancing, pushing my nose into frosty white piles of snow. I was covered in lovely white flakes. I just couldn't believe what this strange cold thing was. I eventually came back in surprised to see that all the snow that had fallen on me had melted, leaving me cold and wet. Dad dried me with a towel, and I lay down in front of the fire. From then on every winter I looked forward to the arrival of snow.

One morning Dad let me off the lead, and I ran ahead as usual. After a short while I heard him whistle so, I turned and ran back and sat down in front of him looking up at his face expectantly. Dad looked down at me, smiled, and said;

"You may be brilliant at understanding what is required when I speak to you or whistle, but what is going to happen when Margaret takes you for a walk? She can't whistle, and she won't shout so we want it to be simple for her to bring you back, don't we? We have two choices ... one, either I can try to teach Margaret how to whistle. Or two, I teach you that you come back to us when I raise my arm, what do you think?"

I continued to look up at him and wagged my tail.

"Yes, that's what I thought," he said,

"Okay, off you go then," I didn't need telling twice, I was off and running across the field in a flash. After I had been running for a while, I thought, "why hasn't he whistled for me to come back?" so I stopped and looked back, dad was standing with one arm up in the air. I thought "oh, that's what he was talking about, I'd better go back."

This went on for a while, but after a bit of practice, we got it just right.

During this time Mum and I were having our midday walks together, but I had to stay attached to the lead as she still didn't know I would come back.

The following weekend dad said,

"Well Lucky, I think it is time for you to show what we can do, Mum is coming out with us today."

We walked up to the field then he let me off the lead, and I ran on, always looking and listening. I heard dad whistle, and I came back and sat down. Mum was very impressed and made a great fuss of me, patting me and saying that I was a good boy. We did that a couple more times and then dad said,

"Right Margaret, Lucky's going to show you something new."

He sent me off, and I ran for a while and then looked back towards him, he had raised his arm, so I hurtled back, at full pace. When I got back, mum said, "Marvellous, well done Lucky what a clever boy!"

Dad said to her,

"Where we go on this walk and what we do is up to you now Margaret, saying to me, walk on Lucky."

What fun we had, I would dash ahead, every time I turned round mum's arm would be in the air so back, I would run, being praised every time. I realised that this training had been for all of us when we were out we always enjoyed the time. There was none of the stress and shouting that I saw between some of the other dogs and their humans.

It was around this time that I went to the vets for that 'castration' that dad had winced about when I was a little pup.

The operation almost cost me my life. Patrick the vet had warned that because of my size he'd have to use a greater amount of anaesthetic and that could lead to problems.

He told dad and mum that following the operation, it would be vital that I keep warm at all costs. So when I got back home the central heating was on and I was snuggled under a blanket.

Just after midnight though, I could feel myself slipping away and very nearly died. During the night I had became so cold after coming round from such a heavy anaesthetic that my body had started to shut down.

Dad found me in this distressing state and did what dad does best - he took immediate action! He got down the floor with me and wrapped the blanket around both of us. He knew his body heat would keep me warm.

Margaret phoned the number for Patrick the vet and told him what was happening. He said that dad was doing the right thing, there was nothing else that could be done for me. Luckily it worked, and in the morning I was fine. dad and I were close before this but somehow an even stronger bond was formed that night.

Chapter 5

Of course, there was always fun at home as well, and sometimes I would do things that defied logic, and that would cause comments about me. I remember one incident which caused everybody who saw it including our neighbours Geoff and Val to make sounds of disbelief.

It was my habit to chase anything that moves. I would run and bark at anything to make it run – cats, squirrels and field mice. I thought I was very quick and agile, in the garden I would run towards little birds that came to feed on Mum's bird table, they always flew away before I got to them, sometimes they would walk on the path, I thought I would get them then but no luck, they could take off and fly faster than I could run. One day when Dad and Mum were talking over the fence to Geoff and Val. I was lying at Dad's feet when I saw a bird on the ground, I ran as fast as I could and as it took off to fly, I sprang up into the air, straight up. I rose, and the bird flew into my mouth. I turned in the air and came down on all fours. As I landed I heard Geoff say I don't believe it, and everybody agreed with him, I trotted up to Dad and put the bird down at his feet it lay there for a minute, then fluttered its wings moved around then flew away.

Dad said,

"There you go, the sign of a good gun dog, he has a soft mouth."

Geoff said,

"Probably just luck, we'd never see anything like that again."

Dad said

"Maybe not, but I will prove to you how soft his mouth is".

He went into the house and came back with an egg and a cup. He called me to him, and while everyone was watching, Dad put the egg in my mouth. I stood there just holding the egg. Dad said to Mum

"Just walk down the gate and call Lucky to you."

This she did, and I trotted down the path to her. I got to her and sat down.

"Now," said Dad "ask him for the egg",

she held out her hand, and I let the egg drop into her hand.

"Amazing," then Geoff said "it's probably hard-boiled,"

"OK, give it back to him," said Dad. Mum did, and Dad called me to him, I went straight back to him, and he took the egg from me. Geoff said he didn't think that proved anything. "No," said Dad "but this does."

He tapped the egg on the edge of the cup and broke it.

"Well, well", said the neighbours. Dad replied,

"I told you he had a soft mouth" then made a huge fuss of me "well done Lucky" he whispered, as he stroked my back.

I tried very hard to jump up and catch birds a few times after that, but I never succeeded. It must have been luck.

Right from when I was a puppy I liked to nibble people's ears. At first, I could only do it when they picked me up. As I got older and bigger, I'd do it from all four legs if they were sitting down or I would rise up on my hind legs to show I was pleased to see them and still get their ears that way.

On one occasion, David's sister Christine came to see us, and I nibbled her ear. Mum said "mind your earrings",

Too late – one gold earring got into my mouth, and I swallowed it. This, of course, caused great consternation, not because of the value but because the sharp parts might cause me harm.

Fortunately the next day it was passed out the normal way. They always picked up after me, but this time the pile of poo had a bright shiny addition to it. They carefully picked out the earring, and it was duly given a thorough washing in Dettol and returned to Christine.

I think she wore it after that and why not – it's a well-known fact that Dettol kills 99% of known germs so that earring was probably the cleanest in the world after that. Dad and Mum would often laugh at that memory. I never hurt anybody's ear, and I know everybody liked me doing it.

At other times Margaret and I had games to play, by now, I was starting to think of her as mum. One of our favourites would involve mum standing outside the back door, with me standing beside her, she would tell me to stay, then she would throw our ball up the long garden towards the gate. As she threw it, she'd say, "1-2-3 Go"! I would run and get it and fetch it back, but instead of giving it straight back I would run past mum into the house around the kitchen and back out again before dropping the ball at her feet. This would be repeated over and over again, mum and I would laugh all the time.

Mum always knew when I was getting tired, so she would pick up the ball and put it away. Then get me a bowl of fresh cool water and make herself a cup of tea. Then I would lie at her feet while she sat in her chair and drank it, I usually got a drop of her tea as well.

When dad got home from work mum would tell him about our game, and I would make it clear that I wanted him to play as well, he always did, and we had a routine of having a game before going on our evening walk.

Sometimes I changed the game when I played ball with dad. I added to the fun by not giving the ball back. Instead, I would run in and out of the kitchen, dodge around him, go back into the garden – in and out of the bushes, up and down the path and do this until he caught me or I decided I would give the ball back. We would chase around until we were both exhausted. This I think was part of being equals, he would always let me make my decisions, that meant I came back to him because I wanted to, not because I was made to, when we played games it was because we both wanted to and both he and mum always knew when I needed to stop.

After all, that running around dad would have a sit-down for a cup of coffee, and I would always get a drink of water and lie down beside him. We would have a special treat; dad would have a digestive biscuit and break it in to four pieces, and share it with me, he never left me out, and he always commented on how gently I took each piece from him. I never snatched anything, two pieces of his favourite biscuit, I felt very special. He said we never have chocolate biscuits because they are not good for you Lucky. Some people have been heard to say that digestive biscuits are not good for dogs, I don't know about that, but dad says all things in moderation, so neither of us ever had a full biscuit and I am always well. I was always full of energy, so after a little while we would go out for our evening walk.

As time went on our walks got longer and more interesting, after we crossed the field we came to a footbridge that passed over a stream, then on to a footpath that led deeper into the countryside. Although dad and mum crossed the footbridge, I discovered that I had an instinctive love of water so I would plunge straight into the stream and just mess about until they called me. Then I would run along the path to catch them up.

The first time we went on that walk I heard dad say that there was a riding school close by and in the afternoon, at about the time we were out walking, the horses were let loose into the fields. "What are horses," I thought, oh boy was I in for a surprise. Suddenly, off to our left we saw a gate open, and about thirty of these huge four-legged animals came hurtling down the slope towards us, then the swung to their left, running down into the valley. I was very excited, and it wasn't often I saw bigger animals than myself. I just turned and ran along the ridge above them, looking down on them as I was running. I thought I could catch them and run with them, but they were so fast, that I couldn't keep up with them.

I heard dad whistle, so I turned and ran back to him. He was still standing where I had left them.

"Well done Lucky, I'm very pleased with you, I was worried that you might try and run down the ridge and not come back when I whistled. Now I know that I can trust you to be off the lead all the time".

We walked along the ridge in the direction that the horses had gone and after a while, I looked down and saw that they had stopped running and they were eating the grass. They seemed to enjoy it which was strange because I only eat grass when I have an upset stomach and I want to be sick. As we walked along, I saw some other animals that I had never seen before, and dad said they were cows and they were eating the grass as well. They certainly appeared much more sedate than those excitable horses.

These walks were excellent, but little did I know that things were going to get even better.

All I knew was that I was finding life had new things to offer every day.

Also, we had a family friend called Tommy Bruce, he would often come to stay. Tommy was an entertainer, and he and dad were often out in the evening. But when Tommy was in he and I became great pals. He had always had dogs himself, and I enjoyed his company.

Chapter 6

I started hearing a new word 'Holiday' I had no idea what this meant, but I kept being told that I would enjoy it. This word holiday sounded good because, in the normal course of things dad would be missing for at least eight hours of the day, and mum for four. Apparently, this was because they both went to something called work. I didn't think that it affected Whiskey and me very much as we seem to sleep for most of the time they were out.

There was some discussion revolving about a cottage in a little place called 'Bothel', which it seemed was near a slightly bigger place called 'Aspatria'. Mum's mum had lived there when she was young, and from there we would travel to lots of places around an even bigger place dad called 'Cumbria'. We would go to Keswick, and then there would be trips to the west coast, Allonby Bay and to dad's sister caravan at Tangle Wood in Silloth. The beach at Allonby Bay was a place I liked, the only thing I didn't like was the way the sea shouted at me when the tide was coming in, I used to shout back at it, but I wouldn't go into the water. Mum and dad found that very strange as I love swimming and they have trouble keeping me out of lakes, ponds, rivers and streams.

It was always great to spend time there with dad's sister Christine, her husband Dennis and their two dogs Sheba and Flash. The three of us dogs loved to chase sticks together.

Flash who was a border collie, was my great pal and I was very proud of him. One day we were on our way from Bothel to Allonby Bay when a local farmer flagged us down. His sheep were out of the field wandering all over the road. Although Flash had no experience of herding sheep, the farmer asked Dennis if he would let Flash help with rounding up the sheep. This might have seemed a somewhat reckless decision but Flash, under Dennis's control, got the job done, amazing as I say Sheba and I were very proud of him.

One time we stayed at a cottage in Thornthwaite, we enjoyed lots of walks in Winlatter Forrest which was just behind the cottage. Sometimes we'd drive into Keswick, and we would all get a treat there. Needless to say, we had to go in separate cars, four adults and three dogs were too many for one car.

There was another occasion when we were on the reverse journey from Allonby Bay to Bothel. As we were getting close to Bothel, we could see some Grouse chicks on the road. We stopped the cars and Dennis who was driving the lead car got out to see what could be done. Dad got himself in position to make any other cars that approached from either direction aware of the delay.

Three of the chicks had unfortunately been run over and killed before we got there but having moved those to the roadside Dennis was able to reunite the others with their mother in the field.

This act of kindness only served to remind me of why I liked and indeed loved these people.

Over the years we travelled to lots of places in that 'Cumbria' Cockermouth, Maryport, Workington even all the way down to Barrow-in-Furness.

We would often go over to another lovely place called the Eden Valley.

We'd head down the A686 running down past Penrith, Edenhall towards Langwathby, where we would turn left on to the B6412 and head deep in to the Eden Valley. On the way we'd pass through places like Winskill, Great Salkeld, Little Salkeld and the hills of Long Meg and her Daughters to their right with Salkeld Dykes and Lazonby Fell to their left. We'd continue on through Glassonby, Lazonby then over the Eden Bridge and up the hill to Kirkoswald and past the church on the right where dad was christened many many years ago.

At Featherstone Hall we had a choice - turn right and sharp left, or as we usually did, bear left past Lacy's garage over the small bridge past The Crown and Black Bull pubs. The small square where the Post Office used to be on the left, turning right up to the left just after The Featherstone Arms.

I know that's an awful lot of information for a dog to remember, but this was dad's favourite road in all the world, and he'd always give a running commentary about when we drive along it. Mum likes this journey too and the places around it. It was soon etched onto my doggy memory (just in case I had to get home by myself sometime!)

We'd always go that way because dad's Auntie Effie and Uncle Peter used to live there and he liked to think of them as he drove to his home village. After we passed the houses on the left at the top of the hill, we would go straight on across the T-junction, following the road down to Renwick.

Chapter 7

One day they didn't go to work and started putting things in the car. Mum said, "Come on Lucky, we are going on holiday".

Dad had left the back of our estate car open, so I ran out and jumped in, not even stopping to say goodbye to Whiskey. She was staying home this time, but Geoff and Val from next door would make sure she'd be well looked after. Dad closed the tailgate and off we went. I remained standing, dad looked in the mirror and saw me and told me to lie down and relax. I did, and after a while, I fell asleep.

I woke up when the car stopped, and dad let me out, putting my collar and lead on. Then he poured water from a bottle into a bowl, and I had a drink. I was glad of it because my mouth was dry from being asleep. Dad said,

"Right it's time for a little walk to stretch our legs"

I looked around as we walked as there were lots of cars parked near us, I wondered why. Dad told me we had parked on somewhere called 'motorway services', Apparently this was a place where humans had a break from driving their metal kennels and enjoyed walkies too.

As we walked, I could hear the sound of traffic moving, dad who always talked to me when we walked said,

"The motorway is busy today with lots of cars".

We climbed a grassy hill and then went over a style into a small wood with a trail leading through it. When we got on the trail dad took my lead off so I could be as free as he was and I trotted on, sniffing at all the strange new smells.

As I walked along I stopped and cocked my leg and 'marked the territory', other passing dogs would know I had been there before them. To make doubly sure I squatted down and emptied my bowels too. As always dad had a little bag ready for this purpose in his pocket. He picked it up and tied up the bag so we could take it back with us. He'd say,

"I wouldn't like to step in that and neither would anyone else".

The trail took us to the far side of the wood where there was a wire fence running along the edge. Through the fence, I could see some fluffy animals eating grass. I moved to the fence and was tempted to go under it, but I heard dads' voice say,

"No Lucky! Those are sheep, and they don't bother us, so we don't bother them, never chase them, or go near them".

I looked up at him, and we walked back the way we had come, I liked the way he spoke to me quiet and patient in everything he said. I followed him happily back to the car.

Mum was already pouring water into my bowl as we got there. She rubbed my head and asked me if I enjoyed my walk. I wagged my tail to show her I had. Dad said

"Lucky did very well, we saw some sheep on the walk, but he made no attempt to chase them". "very good," said mum.

As we drove off I lay down thinking, if this is a holiday I think I'm going to like it.

While I was asleep, we turned off the Motorway and went on to the smaller country roads. We turned left heading down the A66 towards Keswick, passing Penrith cattle market then The Rheghed Centre on the left. There were many interesting places that we passed as we travelled along. Greystoke, made famous by Edgar Rice Burroughs in 1912 through the pages of his book 'Tarzan of the Apes'. You see it's amazing the things a dog can pick up if he listens to the people around him. After a while, we would turn on to the A591 heading down past Skiddaw and go round the back of Bassenthwaite Lake following the road to Bothel to the cottage.

When I woke up I could smell water, not like the water mum puts in my bowl, this was a strong, intense smell of water mixed with fresh air and trees! I looked out of the rear window, as we drove past lots of trees. Through the trees, I could see a large expanse of water. I started to bark excitedly not really knowing why. Mum and dad laughed saying,

"Settle down Lucky, it's all right - that's Bassenthwaite Lake, we're going to take you there tomorrow".

I continued to bark, I always liked to have the last word, dad laughed again saying, pipe down, we should have called you 'last word Harry'. I stopped barking and laid down. It wasn't long before the car came to a stop. Dad opened the boot and said,

"It's OK Lucky this is our holiday cottage."

I jumped out and ran straight through the open door.

I followed mum via the lounge, through the kitchen and into a small back yard with some steps leading to a garden. Mum went up the steps,

"Come on Lucky, see the lovely garden that we have here for you".

I ran up the steps to find a long stretch of grass with a fence and a gate at the end. I loved it, and I ran round in circles only stopping to cock my leg and have a pee against the fence.

When I looked round, I saw that mum had gone down the steps and back into the house, just as dad was putting a bowl of water on the floor for me, I went to it and drank gratefully.

As I was drinking, mum said

"I'll put the kettle on and make a brew."

"Right," said dad, "I'll bring the bags in and get them upstairs".

I followed him as he headed out to the car and traipsed backwards and forwards in and out of the house. There was something important I could help with - important things such as my lead, my ball, my bone, and not forgetting my squeaky toy (I must admit I caused a few delays with that one. I couldn't help it, the thing kept talking to me!).

When he took the bags upstairs, I went up and down the stairs with him. The stairs were very steep, they didn't bother me then, but as the years went by they got harder and harder to climb until after about eleven years I stopped climbing them. I will tell you about that later.

After we'd finished unpacking dad and I went through to the kitchen and found that mum had made us something to eat. It was a lovely day, so we ate outside in the garden. I thought it best to feed myself today as I didn't think mum would appreciate her food going cold. There's a time and a place for getting my own way.

There was an elderly chap living next door, and he spoke to us over the fence while we were eating.

"Yon's a big dog," he said, "Do ee bite"?

I got up and walked over to the fence and put my head over it while wagging my tail. The senior man stroked my head.

"No Lawrence, he doesn't bite, his name is Lucky"

I liked him, mum and dad said he had lived in that house all his life.

From then on Lawrence always made a fuss of me and we remained friends for many years. Mum said she very often couldn't understand a word Lawrence said. Dad said it was a local dialect and not very different to the one he grew up hearing and speaking in a village not too far away.

After tea, we went for a walk round the village.

"So this is Bothel," I thought. It was very quiet, and I liked it, I'd come to know the place very well over the coming years as we went to stay there two or three times a year.

The next day we got up early, had our breakfast then we went out to the car. I saw that dad was carrying a couple of towels. Usually, these were for if it rained when we were out walking. Strange I thought, the sun is shining and no sign of rain. Where I wondered as we got in the car can we be going?

I didn't have to wait long because after driving for about ten minutes I smelt that lovely smell from yesterday, water. I started shouting which I knew they thought of as barking, but I wanted them to stop.

"It's all right Lucky," said dad, "I'm just parking the car then you can go down the slope in front of us and see what you think of Bassenthwaite Lake". This would become my all time favourite place.

Just before dad opened the car, mum said,

"what if he struggles to swim"?

"No problem," said dad, (he was a very strong open water swimmer and had competed in triathlons), "If it comes to it I'll break all the rules and go in and get him".

Then he opened the door, and I ran down the slope and jumped into the lake. I swam in a straight line across the lake, then turned and swam back.

As I climbed out of the water and shook myself, I saw mum and dad waiting on the bank, smiling with towels in their hands. Mum said my swimming was the most marvellous thing she had ever seen,

I felt very proud. Then we walked along the side of the lake, dad picked up a stick and threw it as far out across the lake as he could, and I would run down into the water then swim out, get the stick and bring it back for him, after doing this several times I would get tired so they would call it a day. I'd still go to the water's edge trying to show that I wasn't tired, but they knew. We would get back to the

cottage, very hungry tired and happy. After eating, I usual lay down and went to sleep.

When I woke up, it would be time for our evening walk, through the lanes around the village. No matter where we went our days always started with a trip to Bassenthwaite Lake, and I would swim, it was my holiday, and I loved every minute of it. Even if it poured with rain somehow, there were always dry towels for me, and no matter what the weather I never heard them say that we would not be going to the lake or for a walk, we always went. When we had been for my morning swim, and I was dry and back in the car, mum would say where we would be going that day.

One day she suggested we go to the Solway Firth, Allonby Bay.

"OK why not, let's see what Lucky thinks of the sea," said dad.

Great, I thought, something new, I had no idea where we were going, but I always trusted that I'd have a good time when we got there.

After a short journey along the coast road, we arrived at Allonby Bay. We pulled on to a car park behind what dad said were sand dunes, and we got out of the car. We walked up and over the top of the sand dunes, I could smell something different in the air. I would later know that it was salt carried on the breeze from the sea water. I'll never forget how excited I was to see the sea lapping against the shore. I raced into the water biting at the waves and barking wildly. It was great day, we walked along the beach, I chased sticks and had lots of fun.

Over the following years we went there often, some days were calm when the sun shone, other days in bad weather when the waves went very high and made a lot of noise when they crashed onto the beach. It was as if the sea was shouting at me and it frightened me so I would shout back at it. In future times I would not go in the sea, I just played on the beach.

On one of these trips to Allonby Bay I had a frightening incident, and I have to say it was all my own fault. By now I was completely trusted, and except for this one occasion, I always did what was asked of me (you notice I say asked because dad always treated as an equal).

On this particular day, we'd walked about half a mile along the beach, then, because the tide was coming in, we climbed over the sand dunes at the point we'd got to and came on to a stretch of grassland that we hadn't walked along before. I was wandering along just ahead of mum and dad as I usually did when I saw what I thought was a small lake ahead of me. I took off like a rocket running full pelt towards this great place to swim. I heard dad's voice calling to me to stop and come back, but I thought "I'm in now", so I ignored him. Big mistake! I was going so fast that I was half way across before I stopped. I knew straight away that I was in trouble, it wasn't water it was deep thick mud, worse than that it smelled terrible, it smelled like the filling station where we stopped for petrol and oil.

I tried to get out but I couldn't move my legs, and I was sinking. I was stuck, and it was awful, I was very frightened. Dad was a very powerful man with strong legs and arms from triathlon training so, with no hesitation he broke the rule about letting dogs fend for themselves and ran in after me, the mud was up to his knees, but he got to me. Then he reached down into the mud underneath me and picked me up. Then with a tremendous effort, he carried me to the firm ground. That was very lucky he said, my feet were on the solid ground otherwise we were both sunk.

By now the tide was in so, we walked me back to the sea, and dad and I went in to wash as much of the oily mud off as we could. They were worried about me as they knew about my sensitive skin. I had suffered from eczema throughout my life.

As we walked sedately back to the car, dad said to me,

"You've got to start thinking before you go running headlong into things", he always amazed me by talking to me as though he knew I understood every word he said. Other humans didn't talk to their dogs the way dad spoke to me, and they just didn't seem to have the same faith in their pets as he had in me.

When we got back to the cottage, they gave me a good wash down in the shower with my special shampoo. When I was dry, they put my special skin cream on. As it happened, I didn't suffer any ill effects from my stressful experience.

Sometimes on the way back from the seaside we'd call in for lunch at the Trout Hotel in Cockermouth. Being a clever dog that liked to listen to my knowledgeable dad I'd heard him say a two-leg called Wordsworth had once lived in Cockermouth - he liked to wander around like a daffodil apparently, and his house had been just a few yards away from the hotel. Also, a famous singer called Bing Crosby used to stay at The Trout Hotel when he came over for the fishing. These things weren't really of much interest to me, of course, the main thing about the place for me was that the grounds went down to the river, so more swimming for me!

Sometimes dad's sister Christine and her husband Dennis would pop along to the cottage for a visit. They would bring their dogs Sheba and Flash with them. I liked Christine, Dennis and the dogs, and we rubbed along together very well, so we always had a good time. Having said that Flash was younger than Sheba and I and sometimes he would want to mess about when we were trying to sleep. If he did, I told him off; he was a good lad at heart, so he always listened to me and go off and do something else, leaving Sheba and me to have a kip.

It was around this time that Sheba passed away. I know Flash missed her so much. I was sorry she was gone, she and I had been great pals. It was probably around a year later when another dog came to live with them – a Border Collie called Jess. The three of us got on very well together.

One of the other trips we would make was to the village dad came from. We would visit the farm where dad's childhood friend Robert lived with his wife Linda and their son Edward. I enjoyed myself there, and they had a Labrador called Maple. Maple and I would have great fun running round the farmyard chasing each other.

Sometimes we'd walk through the village round the surrounding lanes out towards another village called Croglin, as we walked he would tell mum and me about his childhood days. I could not have been happier, and I think they both knew it. All in all these holidays were wonderful, and I really enjoyed them. Mind you for me even when we were at home every day was a holiday.

Chapter 8

My relationship with mum and dad was different from the one that Whiskey had with them, because, for her own reasons Whiskey stayed at home and did her own thing, I went nearly everywhere with them, having said that the four of us made a really happy family.

David and Margaret's best friends, Peter and Lynda Leonard often came to our house, They were very nice people, and I liked them, and I could tell that the liked me.

I would stay with them if Margaret and David needed to go away on their own; this would happen once or maybe twice every year. I quite often had a day or so with them, but I occasionally stayed for a week. I really enjoyed being with them, they always made me feel welcome and treated me so well. If I hadn't had dad and mum in my life, I would have happily lived with them all the time.

They gave me a real home from home on these occasions, and Lynda even gave me old shoes to chew.

Peter seemed to be very fond of calling me "Stupid Dog"! This was because he instructed me in a different way than I was used to. I didn't always pick up on what he was saying, so he must have thought that I wasn't very bright. However he said it in an affectionate way, so it didn't stop us having some great walks together, we just got on in a different way.

There was one unfortunate incident that happened one time I was staying at their house. It involved their garden pond, and some fish that I heard were called Coy carp.

I went out in the back garden on the first day of my stay when I reached the corner of the house I turned left into the actual garden and was delighted with what I saw – a fish pond! Without hesitation, I ran forward and jumped in for a swim (I do like a good swim). There was an almighty SPLASH. Water flew up in the air, and the Coy carp were going in every direction. Not one of my better decisions – this time I really had been a stupid dog. I was in big trouble and needed cleaning up.

I decided that in future the Coy carp could have that pond. Peter and Lynda forgave me, but I knew they weren't pleased. Just another case of me acting without thinking, again! A habit I have worked very hard on correcting. However in spite of the mistakes I made from time to time, even when things went wrong, life was still all right.

Despite the supply of chewy old shoes I was always pleased to see dad and mum when they returned and would jump in the car without so much as a 'by your leave' to Peter and Lynda. Nevertheless, I loved them lots and missed them when they later went to live in Spain.

One lovely warm summer day dad and I were out walking along a footpath through the woods, he was wearing shorts and a T-shirt which would later prove to be a mistake. I was off the lead as usual when we saw some youths poking sticks in a hole under the roots of a tree, just as we were coming up to them they dropped the sticks and ran off.

As we walk past I suddenly felt as though I was being stabbed with thousands of needles, I was spinning like a top trying to bite the buzzing things, and ; perhaps know dad was trying to help me but I was almost blind with pain. The pain became too much, so I just turned and ran all the way home, I seemed to keep on being stung all the way. Dad had no chance of keeping up with me, when I got home mum was very worried and asked me where dad was, I couldn't tell her, so she ran out to look for him.

After a while they came back together, dad came in the house and made a fuss of me and told me it was all right, I had been stung by something called wasps. It turned out that his legs and arms had been stung, but he had walked not run, knowing that I would go home. He told us about the time as little boy that he had been stung by wasps all over his face and neck, he said his grandma had put dolly blue all over the stings. Since then he said wasps were no problem to him although, if he had been wearing trousers he wouldn't have got his legs stung.

"Anyway" he said, "Off we go again, we are going to enjoy our walk."

Mum came with us we went back and followed the same footpath.

After a while we were getting back to where the wasps had stung me, so I hung back, I didn't want to go near the place again. Dad stopped turned and spoke to me,

"It's OK Lucky the wasps have gone now they will make another nest somewhere, and we like this walk so we have to get past here or it will spoil the walk".

While he was talking, I suddenly noticed that we had walked past the place where we had been stung and nothing had happened to us. I turned and passed again just to be sure, then I turned and followed mum and dad. I was never stung again but, I never forgot the experience.

We spent many happy years at the place we called home, and I thought things would never change. Then one day in 2002 mum got a phone call and ran out suddenly, and I didn't know why that was. Dad had had a serious accident, and he had to stay away for a while to get better. Eventually, he came home on two things called crutches and for several weeks he was unable to go out for walks with me. Mum took me but, I couldn't wait to get home, it was no fun without dad. From then on whenever we went out again he leant heavily on a stick and couldn't go far. He'd been told that he'd never be fit for work again and things would never be the same. On the plus side, we were still good companions who took care of each other plus it meant that dad was home all the time and we went everywhere together.

We still went away to the cottage and of course I would enjoy many more trips to Bassenthwaite Lake, and happy, lazy afternoons in the garden at the the cottage in Bothel. Of course, we still made the trips out to Renwick in the Eden Valley to see Robert and Linda, but we didn't go for long walks anymore. Dad was in constant pain, but he still took me out letting me mooch around, although I never wandered too far from him. I was slowing down myself, not running blindly after things when I did as a pup, I'd started just watching cats and squirrels not feeling the inclination to chase them anymore.

By now we had all slowed down our pace of life. After all, I was nearly eleven years old. Some people would be heard to mutter:

"What a big dog, they don't usually live past eight or nine years of age". Dad said

"We don't listen to that we just live every day and enjoy it",

So we did. Even Whiskey was slowing down; we weren't entirely sure how old she was, (you know how ladies can be about their age), she wouldn't even tell me. But she was probably at least two years older than me.

The first thing we noticed was that she didn't see as well as she had. This meant she stopped climbing trees in the garden, and never left the garden, content to wander in and out of the flower beds. If the sun was warm, she'd lie down and go to sleep on the garden bench. The days when we chased each other around were gone. I liked to be with her so if she lay down and went to sleep I would lie down close to her and we would both have a nap.

We were spending more and more time up in Cumbria; the big difference was that I found the stairs difficult so instead of going up to the bedroom at night, I slept downstairs. Getting up the steps to the garden at the back wasn't easy, so mum and dad started to talk about making changes. Dad couldn't get upstairs very easily either because of his leg problems so they decided we would give up the cottage and move to a more suitable location. It was a sad occasion when we closed the door of the cottage for the last time.

The place we chose to go to gave us a couple of very happy years, and as it wasn't too far from Bothel, we could still call on Lawrence the elderly chap who lived next door at the cottage. Unfortunately, he wasn't getting any younger, and he was suffering poor health.

By now dad and mum had found a nice Holiday Lodge to stay in. It was a wooden bungalow with a railed veranda which we would sit out on in the evenings. Located on the edge of Skiddaw View Caravan Park it was in a lovely location. It had two bedrooms so Christine, Dennis and their dogs could still come and stay with us. It became home from home just like the cottage had been. We were still able to have our trips out, but our trips to Bassenthwaite Lake were becoming fewer. Although I still loved to swim, because I had arthritic hips I would take a couple of days to recover from my exertions. Eventually, we just stopped going; I missed it, but I knew it was the right decision.

Around this time we had a very sudden and for me an unexpected shock. This was a very sad event and made a big change to our lives, after being very poorly one day Whiskey just lay down and died during the night. Mum and dad were very upset, and so was I, Whiskey was part of our family, and we missed her. She was buried in Christine and Dennis's garden. I wondered why she wasn't buried in our garden, but I soon found out.

One day we packed everything up, and I heard David and Margaret say that we were moving house. Two of our friends Roy and his wife Paula, arrived with a big van and a lot of our stuff was packed in it. When it was full, we got in the car, and Roy drove the van with Paula in the passenger seat. Imagine my surprise and delight when we reached our destination, Renwick the village where dad was born and brought up.

We would be making a new home there, living in a converted barn. We all loved our surroundings, and new people were coming to call, and they all seemed to like me. We settled into a new routine, with walks, a complete change of scene and tempo, and we were all very happy. We all missed Whiskey and wished that she could still have been with us.

Chapter 9

One of the first big changes to our routine came about almost as soon as we moved in. Dad had grown up working with cows, so when he got settled back into the village, he asked Robert if he could do anything to help with his cattle. Robert said he could give a try and feed them in the Low Yard. Dad was delighted because he had spent the last couple of years with people telling him he wasn't able to do anything. He knew he was slow and that he had reached retirement age but just wanted to feel useful once more.

The Low Yard was about five minutes hobble away from our front gate leaning on his stick. In his prime, dad would have covered the distance in a few seconds, but now he was just pleased to take his time and have something to do.

The new routine involved dad getting up at 5.30am leaving mum asleep in bed and coming downstairs to me. I slept downstairs in front of the fire. Dad would open the front door, and I would wander into the garden and relieve myself. When we went back in he would make a slice of toast and a cup of coffee, we always shared the toast. After his drink, dad would go and tend to the cows, and I'd stay with mum. He didn't think it was a good idea for me to be around cattle in a closed environment when I hadn't grown up around them.

Even though dad was a bit of a slowcoach Robert said he was good with the cattle, even when they were calving they were comfortable having him around. Dad's quiet ways always had a calming influence. It probably took him about an hour longer to feed the cattle than it would have taken Robert, but he enjoyed it, and always said it was worth the extra pain he suffered while doing it.

When he'd get back home, I'd be waiting at the door for him, and he would take me out for a short walk. We were usually back by about 8.30am, and dad would make mum some breakfast. While he was doing that mum would come downstairs and join us. She always fed the wild birds in the garden before coming back in and having her breakfast.

Then mum and dad would sit down listening to the wireless, chatting and reading. Dad's a bit of an author and would often work on his latest book. Life was good for all of us, and we were relaxed and content.

One of the things that dad enjoyed was going to the cattle markets with Robert. They went on a Monday and Wednesday to either Penrith or Carlisle. The trip to Penrith would be along the roads I knew well going out through Kirkoswald, KO as we knew it. Then we would go over the River Eden Bridge and out through Lazenby.

Going to Carlisle was a new experience taking us through and past lots of places that I had never seen before. We went out through Croglin on the B6413 by Newbiggin, Cumrew, Cumrew Fell, cutting across from Castle Carrock to the A69 over Warwick Bridge on though into Carlisle. For a man who spent so many years away from home, working away dad certainly knew his way around. Of course, he walked everywhere when he was young, and you learn a lot about an area when you are on foot. As he said he very often didn't know what a road was called, but he knew where it went. One day we even went to a place called Brampton, I never knew why we went there, but I always enjoyed the trips out.

Sometimes we went out of the village and turned on to the A686 to see friends in Gamblesby and Melmerby. On other occasions, we went out to the right up by Hartside Heights and Gilderdale Forest on the same road to see friends in Alston.

A trip dad and Robert always enjoyed because of their mutual love of horses, was a drive out to Hexham race course. We would go out on the A686 past Alston Ninebanks, Whitfield, Allen Banks and Starward Gorge, turning on to B6305 at Langly, past West Dipton Burn to Hexham.

Every day was an adventure, and I was sharing dad's trip down memory lane.

One day a few weeks after we had moved into our new home I thought a tornado had hit the house, a whirling dervish in the form of a black Labrador bitch called Bonnie had come to visit. Bonnie was the pet of Chris, a friend of dad and mum he was an electrician and it had been decided that sometimes, more often than not, in fact, he would leave Bonnie with us while he went to work.

Bonnie was lots of fun and very lively, sometimes too lively for a venerable 13-year-old like me. Somehow she always knew when I was getting tired. We spent the next two years sharing our walks with Bonnie and helping dad to train her for his friend. Bonnie was a clever dog, and she instinctively understood the word 'no'. She concentrated better than I did at the same age. Dad was kind enough to say she took her example from me and that I was a big help in getting her to understand his instructions. These were great days so when dad told me that his friend Chris was emigrating to Spain and that Bonnie would be coming to live with us I was very pleased.

As happy as I was I had no way of knowing that this idyllic life was coming to an end, I would be parted from dad and mum, and I would have to leave our lovely home, and I never saw Bonnie again. But I am getting ahead of myself we had many happy days, weeks and months still in front of us, friends of many years standing would be coming to visit and stay with us. Roy and Paula, who helped us move, Joan and Pat, Dave and Anne who always brought their dog Candy with them, even Peter and Lynda who now lived in Spain came to see us. These were indeed the best of times.

I told you early in the book about how much I loved snow, but nothing could have prepared me for snow in the Eden Valley. Dad had talked about being trapped in the village in the forties and fifties during the winter, but the first morning I saw it I was amazed.

When dad opened the front door, the snow fell inside. I looked out, and the snow was higher than our garden wall. He had to get a shovel and clear a path to the gate. There was only one road running through the village, and it was full of snow. Dad, of course, had to get to the Low Yard which was even more of a struggle than usual for him to get there. It took him a long time, but he made it after all cattle need feed rain or snow.

A little later a farmer from the far end of the village drove down in his big tractor, and this flattened the snow. Making it hard packed. I was pleased about this because it also meant that dad and I could still have our walk later.

The flattened snow had it's own problems because when the temperature dropped the snow would freeze and it became very slippery underfoot. Still, this is a small price to pay for living in, as dad always called it 'Gods own country'. It was the best of places.

In spring and summer the rich brown soil freshly ploughed, was so different from the soil in other places. The crops and foliage so much greener and you would have to be an artist to describe the changing colours in autumn. If you are lucky enough to live any part of your life in the Eden Valley then, you truly have been blessed by God.

However, it seems nothing in life is meant to last forever and our days in paradise were coming to an end.

The day things began to change forever began in the usual way. Because dad had a great sense of responsibility, he always made sure he did the things that should be done, without fail.

I never once saw him fail to do the right thing so although I had noticed for a few days things were not right with him I couldn't have anticipated what was to come. It was nothing specific, maybe more pain, the pain and worry were clearly etched on his face.

Dad was up at 5.30am just as he always did, I went in the garden, as usual, then we had our toast, dad had his coffee and then went to see to the cattle as normal. At this time mum was still asleep in bed, so all was as it should be.

As usual, dad arrived back from feeding the cattle and took me for my short walk. The change to our routine started when we returned. Mum was up and dressed, and she had already had her breakfast.

I couldn't understand why but on this morning they just kept moving around. Dad started putting few things in the car. When he had finished, dad came and got me into the car as I couldn't jump in with a single bound as I did in my youth. Mum came out of the house and got in the car too then we set off. I thought it was just another trip like so many we had taken before, so I lay down.

We drove slowly out of the village. When we got to the top of the hill, dad stopped, paused and looked down on the village behind us, saying to mum,

"I don't know if I'll ever be able to come back here again".

"Of course you will" mum replied, "They'll sort you out, and we will be back in a week or so".

"Maybe" dad replied, "I'm not so sure".

They sounded so sad, and this was not like them. The only time I had sensed sadness like this was when Whiskey died. Then I fell asleep and apart from them stopping for one comfort break we didn't stop until I found we had arrived in Manchester outside our friends Joan and Pat's house.

Chapter 10

Joan and Pat are old friends of ours; I mentioned them earlier when the came to stay in Renwick with us. Joan was one of the first people to see me after mum and dad got me. They had also been next door neighbours before I came along I was always pleased to see them. One of my earliest friends had been their dog, a Rottweiler called Rocky, sadly Rocky was no longer with us.

Before we went into the house, dad took me for a quick walk, when we came back, we went into the kitchen, and I had a drink of water. Mum had given Joan and Pat a carrier bag which contained my bowls and my food; there was enough for week mum said. After sitting and talking with Joan and Pat for a while mum and dad got up saying we will be back to see you after the examination. They went out of the house leaving me behind. I barked and complained, but Joan and Pat were kind making a fuss of me. Then Pat said,

"Don't worry Lucky your mum and dad will be back soon".

I settled down and waited. Several days passed, Joan took me out for walks, but always on the lead, I watched and waited, but there was no sign of mum and dad returning.

Then after a week had passed by suddenly a knock on the door. It was mum and dad, and I was very excited and pleased to see them. Dad took me straight out for a walk. I could see he was struggling and leaning heavily on his stick. He looked very sad, and I didn't know how to cheer him up. He talked to me all the time,

"Lucky you are a wonderful dog, you have been a loving and loyal companion, I am so sad that I may not see you again".

I was so happy to see him but confused by what he said. Before we got back to the house, he said,

"I have loved you and cared for you just as I would have if you had been my son".

We went back into the house, and both dad and mum made a fuss of me, then they left.

That would be the last time I ever saw dad.

A few days later mum came and picked me up, Christine's husband Dennis was driving the car, but there was no sign of dad, and mum

was very tearful. She sat in the back with me and made a fuss of me all the way back to Christine and Dennis's house. As we travelled along, I was sure I'd see dad soon. When we arrived Dennis stopped the car, and we all got out, I looked to see dad coming out, but there was no sign of him.

Christine and the two dogs, Flash and Jess, were at the gate and they were very pleased to see me, but I avoided them. There was only one person I wanted to see and went through the door into the house sure that I would find him there. There was no sign of him anywhere; I went from room to room, but dad simply wasn't there. I lay down and watched and waited for him to come, but he never came.

I would hear conversations in which dads name was mentioned, but I couldn't understand what they were saying, I heard words like 'terrible' and 'awful' and 'surely somebody can do something', comments that I assumed were something to do with dad, but I just couldn't understand.

After a few weeks, I started to think, this must be like Whiskey, and that dad had died. As I convinced myself of this, I was filled with despair. My only thought was that if I too died then I will see him again, with this in mind, I laid down and stopped moving. I didn't eat my food or drink water, and I just waited for the end.

Mum tried to help me as did Dennis and Christine, but I was beyond help. Mum called the vet out in the hope that he would get me back on my feet. After examining me and just shook his head saying,

"I have only seen this very rarely, and I don't know why but this dog has simply lost the will to live."

Mum said, "After 16 years of being with him Lucky is waiting for my husband to come home, but he can't, for health reasons we don't know when he will be home and Lucky misses him".

Then the vet said, "Lucky is clearly dying from a broken heart."

"He may last a couple of days at most, but we can't bring him back from this".

mum said, "It is so cruel, I can't bear to see him suffer like this".

The vet replied, "The kindest thing to do would be to put him to sleep". Mum tearfully agreed. Then the vet said he is such big dog; perhaps I should muzzle him before I get the needle ready. Mum refused,

"You are not demeaning him like that, he is the gentlest dog who ever lived", she held me in her arms and told me that she loved me and that dad loved me, I never felt anything I just slipped away.

The End

Final word from Dave Lodge (dad)

This is the end of Lucky's story, but speaking as his friend and companion for 16 years I have to say that no more loyal dog ever lived. We did everything together throughout his life.

For my part, I have no hesitation in telling you that, from the moment he came into our lives, Lucky, Margaret and I enjoyed many happy days. They were joy filled days, precious memories that flood back as I share these recollections with you. We did always share Digestive Biscuits - they were our favourite.

We found Lucky dumped on the verge on the Mancunian Way the very busy elevated motorway that runs through the heart of Manchester. He had obviously been thrown from a moving car and was very fortunate to not have suffered major injuries. This event had a lasting effect for a long time afterwards - whenever the car we were travelling in came to a stop he'd have a tendency to be sick ... of course we were aware of this and were always well prepared with reassuring words and towels. He eventually overcame this fear with great patience, trust and understanding from both sides.

I had a different feeling about what happened on some occasions. So I will just tell you of some of his stories from my point of view.

When he ran into the foul smelling bog at Allonby Bay, I was reckless in the extreme when I ran in and picked him up. I had no idea how deep it was or if I could get out of it.

As Margaret said, I broke every rule I ever spoke about concerning rescuing dogs from the situations they sometimes get in to. My excuse was that Lucky was our friend, and so I reacted as I would if Margaret or a dear friend found themselves in similar trouble, I just plunged in. All I knew was I didn't want anything to happen that would cause me to be without my great companion.

Having said that, my advice is that you should not do what I did. Dogs have great survival instincts, and there are many cases of people jumping into rivers to save their dog and drowning, the dog then being found safe on the bank, later in the day.

Other incidents such as being stung by a nest of wasps, In that I can only praise Lucky for having the good sense to leave the area with great haste. More sense than me at the age of seven when a wasps nest fell on me from a crab apple tree. I was dancing on the spot, complaining to the man who came to my aid,

"Ee Lol, these flies have got hot feet"!

Lucky would not have been that silly he knew that the best thing to do was get home.

Indeed in my eyes he was a most remarkable dog who had no limit to his capabilities. He was very agile in his youth and did jump up and catch a bird in flight. He was so gentle as you have read, he could even carry an egg in his mouth without breaking it.

These traits enriched the lives of all the people who knew him. He is still spoken of in glowing terms many years after he passed away.

How many of us can truly claim to have achieved that kind of admiration in our life time? We continue to strive for the levels of loyalty, friendship and love that Lucky achieved. He will always be missed but never forgotten.

Following the accident that left me dependent on a walking stick, I was unable to leave the house. He was my constant companion and never complained about missing his three daily walks. Then when I could get out again, he matched my slow pace and never ran off or left me. Indeed, the reason I recovered to the level of fitness I did was because I didn't want to let Lucky down; so this encouraged me to walk as far as I could with him.

In the later account when I had to spend a prolonged time in the hospital, something had poisoned my system. The doctors never found out what it was. I was on various intravenous drips for nutrition, hydration and antibiotics as I could stomach neither food nor water. When I took Lucky for what did turn out to be his last walk with me and told him what a great dog he had been, I knew in my own heart that I was sinking fast and truly believed, that I would never recover from what ailed me.

There was no way Lucky would have been able to understand that, he would only know that his companion of many years was gone. So I do believe as the vet said that he gave up and died of a broken heart. I am very sad that I inadvertently became the cause of shortening his life.

He will continue to live in my heart till the day I die.

People who believe in reincarnation have suggested that Lucky has returned to us. I don't know enough about the subject of reincarnation to be sure that such things are possible; however, there are times when our latest family member Bruno cocks his head to one side and looks at me I feel I am seeing someone I have known before.

Lucky passed away at 1pm on the 20th August 2009. He was an intelligent and thoroughly lovely dog. His loss affected us deeply, and we missed him immensely. Filled with sadness, we started to reminisce about the adventures we shared and jotted them down. This book is the result.

I leave it up to you to decide the answer to the question Lucky asked at the start of his book:

"A dog can have a life story can't he"?

Lucky lived a great life in a wonderful way, and his story deserved to be told. I think that those of you who have shared their lives with a Lucky of your own will agree with me.

We have always been avid dog lovers. Our current adopted family member is a bouncy German Shepherd Cross called Bruno. I'm sure he and Lucky would have liked each other and been great pals. Bruno came to us from the Dogs Trust at Darlington and £1 from every book sold will be donated to the trust.

David, Margaret and Bruno in 2016

Whiskey the cat

With Dad at Kirkoswald Church

Me with a chew stick nomnom

Me at 6 months old

On the sofa with Mum and Christine

My friend Flash

My friend Jess

My friend Sheba

With Flash at Thornthwaite

Bassenthwaite Lake

The cottage at Bothel

With Sheba at Bassenthwaite Lake

With Flash at the Trout Hotel

Dennis & me

Lucky's Scrap Book

THE LONG ROAD — Dave Lodge

ONE MAN'S EPIC JOURNEY THROUGH THE WORLD OF SPEEDWAY, SPORT AND SHOWBUSINESS

Starting from the rural backdrop of Cumbria, as a young man, Dave ventured South to Manchester. There he was involved in Speedway at the world famous Belle Vue track, he played Rugby for TocH, and competed in Marathons, Triathlons and even Quadrathons! In 1973 a chance meeting with Tommy Bruce, the sixties rock 'n' roll star, started him on a path into the world of showbusiness. As manager and promoter for Tommy, Dave mixed with the great rock 'n' rollers from the Sixties and the world of entertainment of the day. This book is a warm recollection of these times, a celebration of the people behind the celebrity – never in a negative or salacious way, simply a reflection of the warmth, camaraderie and teamwork of the people he encountered whether on a Speedway Track, a Rugby field, a Marathon or Backstage.

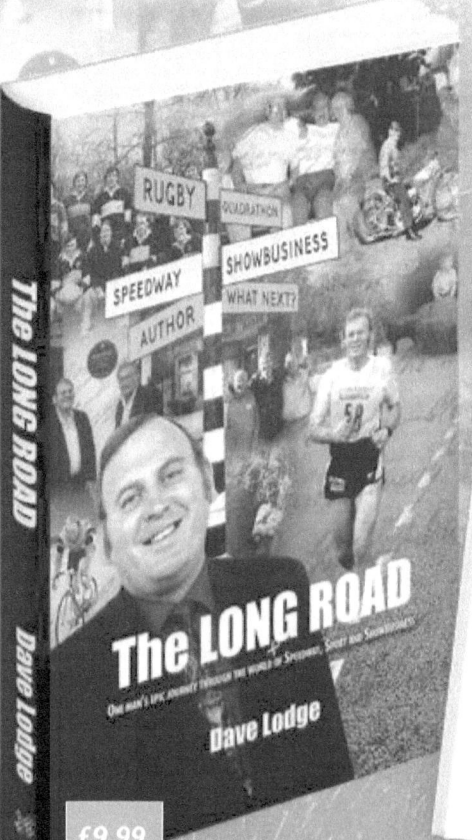

£9.99

Paperback: 360 pages / over 300 B&W photos
ISBN-13: 978-0-9934679-4-3
Available from local bookshops, Amazon & Bertrams
or directly from the author at: davelodgeauthor@gmail.com

Pixel tweaks
PUBLICATIONS
ULVERSTON · CUMBRIA
WWW.PIXELTWEAKSPUBLICATIONS.COM

Also by Dave Lodge

Have Gravel, will Travel
The Official Tommy Bruce Biography

The amazing story of how a young cockney lad went from 'barra boy' to a teen singing idol. A unique insight into the 1960's rock 'n' roll scene when Tommy Bruce and contemporaries such as Billy Fury, Johnny Kidd and Joe Brown were doing the rounds together. In this fickle world of show business many friendships don't stand the test of time. Not so that of Tommy Bruce and Dave Lodge, his manager, friend and author of this biography. We see how their partnership has endured since the 1960's unhampered by contracts, surviving on friendship through the highs and lows. The book is a testimony to Tommy's affable style both on and off stage making him a well-loved character in the industry for the past five decades.

Price: £6.99

Paperback: 280 pages / 100 B&W photographs
Publisher: Pixel Tweaks Publications (July 2015)
ISBN-13: 978-0992751487

www.ingramcontent.com/pod-product-compliance
Lightning Source LLC
Chambersburg PA
CBHW020623300426
44113CB00007B/765